LAURENCE FREEMAN OSB

# *The Goal of Life*

EXCERPTS
FROM
*Jesus the Teacher Within*

*Revised by Liam Kelly*

**CONVIVIUM**PRESS

MEDITATIO

2 0 1 2

*The Goal of Life*

© Laurence Freeman OSB

© Convivium Press 2012
All rights reserved
For the English Edition

http://www.conviviumpress.com
sales@conviviumpress.com
convivium@conviviumpress.com

7661 NW 68th St, Suite 108,
Miami, Florida 33166. USA.
Phone: +1 (305) 8890489
Fax: +1 (305) 8875463

Edited by Rafael Luciani
Revised by Liam Kelly
Designed by Eduardo Chumaceiro d'E
Series: *Meditatio*

ISBN: 978-1-934996-30-0

Printed in Colombia
Impreso en Colombia
D'VINNI, S.A.

Convivium Press
Miami, 2012

*The Goal of Life*

# Contents

# The Goal of Life

In my book «Jesus, the Teacher Within», I take the central question of Jesus, «Who do you say I am?», and I explore this question in many aspects. In these extracts from that book, from Chapter 10, I refer in particular to the experience of meditation. How does meditation, deepening our Christian faith, help us to listen to, understand, and respond to this central question of Jesus?

1

Let's begin with that section of Chapter 9 of St Luke where we hear this question put to us.

> «One day, when he had been praying by himself in the company of his disciples, he asked them, "Who do the people say I am?" They answered, "Some say John the Baptist, others Elijah, others one of the prophets of old has come back to life". And "You", he said, "who do you say I am?" Peter answered, "God's Messiah". Then he gave them strict orders not to tell this to anyone. He said, "The Son of Man has to endure great suffering and be rejected by the elders, chief priests

and scribes, to be put to death and to be raised up again on the third day". To everybody he said, "Anyone who wants to be a follower of mine must renounce self. Day after day, he must take up his cross and follow me. Whoever wants to save his life will lose it, but whoever loses his life for my sake will save it. What does anyone gain by winning the whole world at the cost of his true self?"».

2

To be able to say who Jesus is, we need to know who we ourselves are. How well we can see and recognize him in his spiritual body depends upon the clarity and depth of our self-knowledge.

3

The goal of life —it can be called «heaven», «nirvana», «liberation», «salvation» or «enlightenment»— is to know fully who we are. Self-transcendence is the way to self-knowledge. In this state the centre of consciousness no longer resides in the ego. From the deeper centre of the true self, we are conscious of union with others within our uniqueness rather than separation. There are not many gods but one God, not many selves but one Self, one True I am in which all beings share in Being.

4

Individual identity is not lost when we know ourselves, but it is transcended. We are freed of its inherent illusions of self-sufficiency and self-centredness. This individuality is lost by letting go of it. The true Self then becomes clear. There are not many individual enlightenments as the ego may imagine but the one great enlightenment of the Self in which all participate. And, because self-knowledge cannot be encapsulated in any mental concept or image or psychic or psychological happening, there is no single, universal definition of the Self. No definition can express the lightning flash of insight into the ordinary which awakens self-knowledge.

14

The process through which self-knowledge arises embraces the whole spectrum of our life-experience. All forms of love and all relationships, work and play, physical, mental and psychological growth, creativity and frustration, good and evil, vice and virtue, grief and joy, loss and gain —all invite the self-transcendence which leads to liberation from our habitual submersion in ego.

To co-relate all these experiences and make them fully conscious, all religious traditions have recognised the essential value of meditation. This means the simplifying practice of silence and stillness, of non-action beyond thought and imagination, the stilling of the activities of the mind. Integrated into ordinary life, the practice of meditation harmonises and integrates in the spirit all that we think and feel and say and do.

The word «meditation» has acquired a variety of meanings in western tradition. The *meditatio* of the desert monks meant simply a prayer of the heart, a kind of chewing over or repetition of a piece of scripture or the Word. By the seventeenth century it had come to mean almost exclusively an organised method of cerebral prayer employing intellectual analysis and visual imagination. In the East there are also many kinds of meditation but they usually refer to a non-discursive, silent practice beyond thought and imagination. Here I am using the word «meditation» in its non-discursive sense roughly synonymous with contemplation. One could say that meditation is the work we do to accept the gift of contemplation which is already given and present in the heart.

In both Western and Eastern traditions, meditation (or contemplation) is acknowledged as an essential work, an ongoing discipline of the pilgrimage of spiritual growth. In one sense it is both means and end. Meditation reconciles the contradictions and opposites which run across the spectrum of human wholeness. Prayer is the deepest, the primal therapy of the suffering human condition. Therefore meditation («pure prayer») is not an elite practice for the spiritually advanced. It is the natural way to grow.

9

Nor is meditation the get-away-from-it-all narcissistic indulgence which advertising posters trendily proclaim to the stressed and hyperactive commuters of the Western (and increasingly the Asian) world. The spiritual journey involves the need and desire to meditate. It is a universal practice although each individual, like each spiritual tradition, appropriates it in his or her own way.

10

Meditation is not leisure activity—though it takes time and requires relaxation. From a spiritual perspective you relax in order to meditate rather than meditating just in order to relax.

11

You can survive without meditation. But it is the wind in the sail of the soul. If life is more than survival, if life is about growth, flourishing, integration, then meditation is necessary. It is a work that harmonises the usually discordant dimensions of our consciousness.

ଔ

18

Its fruits are agreed on by all traditions. They need little definition or defence: compassion and wisdom, generosity and tolerance, forgiveness and kindness, gentleness and peace, joy and creativity —in other words, happiness and simple, basic human goodness. By liberating these potential qualities, meditation advances the cause of human wholeness. It illustrates in real life that holiness is not just about interiority. To be good means simply to have the inner and the outer dimensions of ourselves in union, to be in harmony with our true nature. Because this wholeness is the spirit, meditation opens everything we do to the spiritual dimension. With regular practice, meditation thus establishes a deeply satisfying and peaceful consistency within ourselves and between ourselves, others and all the activities of our lives.

# From Relationship to Union

In exploring this question of Jesus, «Who do you say I am?» I have come to feel that the important thing about the question is that we learn to listen to it. Not merely coming up with the right answer or many answers, but that we really learn to understand through listening, and that we are changed through this listening.

1

I want to turn to meditation to explore how we can listen to this question in the deepest possible way. We will then see that meditation is a way of silence and self-transcendence, a way of relationship and solitude, a way to read without words, to know without thought. Through self-knowledge the meditator is brought to the threshold of the knowledge of God within a relationship with Jesus. This relationship with Jesus asks nothing of us except the total gift of self. Meditation, in the light of Christian faith, is a deepening encounter with the mind of Christ. We meet the Risen Jesus even if we do yet fully recognize or name him.

## 2

Meditation inaugurates a whole new way of being. It is much less a technique than a way of life. It is initiated by the gradually emergent experience of communion, oneness with self and others that reaches beyond the boundaries of all dualistic relationships. Although most people are passionately interested in their relationships and see them as the most sacred element of their lives, relationships as such are but a stage on the human journey.

## 3

Beyond relationship —at the silent heart of every relationship, where the walls dividing us crumble— is union. In relationship we are always looking at a separate other. The looking at, the distance implied in that objectification of the other person, creates the suffering inherent in all relationship. It is the suffering of conflict arising from the ego's desire to possess and control. It is the suffering too of the eventual and unavoidable loss of the one we love. In union, however, there can be no possessiveness because desire itself has been transcended. Egotistical boundaries are dissolved. Uniqueness embraces uniqueness and finds selfhood in otherness, sameness in difference. Fear and desire, domination and submission are ended. What is gained is more than desire ever fantasised. When human relationships, rarely and usually briefly, touch this degree of fullness they can truly be called spiritual friendship. They realise their destiny and potential as ways of sharing through the Spirit in the divine community of love. In union otherness is shared, entered into, absorbed rather than externalized. We are within the other and they are within us.

4

All this is the fruit of meditation. The seed of union lies in our nature, now, waiting to be germinated. Meditation accepts the invitation of this potential and prepares us for the death which growth demands. All this is important to grasp before starting to meditate. Understanding this saves unnecessary false starts and moderates impatience. It helps us see that the place we should look for the fruits of meditation is not the meditation period itself —what «happens» (or doesn't)— but in the manner and quality of our lives, particularly our relationships. We are not looking for anything extraordinary to happen in meditation. The point is to see the presence of God in the ordinary, to transform our perception of reality, not to recreate the world to conform to our plans or to enter into a «other kind of world» way of living. It is not an escape from life's problems. It is not easy. But it is —and this is the most important aspect of meditation to see clearly— utterly simple. The joy and the peace beyond understanding that results is what happens.

5

Meditation is concerned not so much with our relationship to God as with our union with God. This does not mean that all relationship with God (together with the ideas, images and dialogue involved in relationship) is thereby ended. The idea of relationship continues to be a necessary framework of coming to meaning and decisions. It remains an important language of life. Relationship endures as long as we continue to utter or think in terms of our own «I», that is until the end of time. But relationship is also changed radically by meditation. The language of relationship is enhanced and rendered more meaningful. Our knowledge and love of God no longer stop short at the stage of relationship but, as all love wishes to do, pushes on towards complete union. Meditation radically changes the way we understand God. The immediate consequence of this deepening of relationship in communion is felt in human relationships. It is perceptible too in the way we feel part of the natural world. The humanity of Jesus and his relationship to the universe come to be experienced from within. The change undergone in all these dimensions is often described as a coming home. Home to ourselves and to our innate capacity for transcendence.

6

Meditation is of great importance for the modern world. Meditation is such an important source of hope and vision for the next millennium. The recovery of its contemplative tradition is the source by which Christianity is renewed. Out of its crisis a contemplative Christianity will join other faiths as a mediator of compassionate action and healing wisdom to the world.

7

Through the recovery of the practice of meditation, religion and spirituality, which are moving apart rapidly at present, can be re-harmonised. After all, religion and spirituality share a common goal of uplifting the human spirit. Deeper spirituality means deeper prayer. And the health of religion is the quality of its prayer life. To find depth we must return to the life-giving roots of the tradition. Something ancient must be embraced as something new so that a contemporary way of seeing Jesus, of listening to his question and of saying who he is, can be born. His question is intrinsic to our culture's search for meaning, peace and justice, and the good life. It also speaks wisely to all that today we understand by the terms self-awareness, self-fulfilment, and transcendence. His question can help guide that search for modern people provided we can find the silence from which to listen to it.

8

The Christian tradition was born in the first experience of the risen Jesus. It is perennially renewed by its return to the roots of that experience. To understand the Christian meaning of meditation we need to see firstly how it is grounded in the teaching of Jesus. The essential elements of meditation are to be found in his great teaching on prayer in the Sermon on the Mount.

# The Lord's Prayer

His disciples once asked Jesus to teach them to pray as John the Baptist had taught his disciples. In reply Jesus gave them a short collection of phrases similar to the Eighteen Benedictions and the *Kaddish* of the synagogue liturgy.

«Our Father, who art in heaven, holy is your name. May your kingdom come and your will be done on earth as it is in heaven. Give us this day our daily bread and forgive us our transgressions as we forgive those who transgress against us. Lead us not into temptation and deliver us from evil».

1

The «Our Father» sums up Jesus' advice that prayer should be sincere, direct and brief. He is adamant that the self-dramatising of the ego should be abandoned. Some scholars believe that, translated back into the original Aramaic, this prayer is a collection of short rhythmic phrases summarizing the content and style of the teaching of Jesus in a style typical of the rabbinical teachers of his day.

The phrases would have been memorised and repeated frequently and interiorly. From the beginning of the Church innumerable commentaries on the Lord's Prayer have seen in it the key to his teaching about prayer and taken it as a starting point for an ever-deepening theology of prayer. To pray the Our Father requires more than the mechanical repetition or chanting of the words. It requires mindfulness. Some commentators have suggested it should never take less than three minutes to recite it. Simone Weil discovered in her way of reciting the Lord's Prayer that it requires attention through a faithful repetition that leads to stillness and insight.

2

In Chapter Six of St Matthew's gospel, the setting in which Jesus taught this formula also emphasises attention as the primary quality of all prayer. His teaching distils the essential elements of meditation. Jesus is a teacher of the contemplative way. Firstly, he emphasises how prayer must be rooted in the sincerity of the true Self rather than in the ego's self-consciousness:

> «Be careful not to make a show of your religion before men; if you do, no reward awaits you in your Father's house in heaven».

Whenever we find security or take pleasure in the approval of others the authenticity of prayer is compromised. Its motivation becomes impure. Good deeds performed in the desire for public recognition lack virtue. To purify the «ground of our beseeching», as Mother Julian calls it, Jesus recommends solitude and interiority, the silent intimacy and the hidden mystery of the prayer of the heart:

> «When you pray, go into a room by yourself, shut the door and pray to your Father who is there in the secret place; and your Father who sees what is secret will reward you».

As a private room would have been a great luxury in Jesus' time, his focus is not so much on domestic arrangements as on the orientation of the mind and heart at the time of prayer. Even the ascetical practices of prayer, such as fasting, he taught, should be performed in a discreet and modest way. They are not solemn ways of feeling holier or bargaining positions in a struggle to get what we want out of God. «I'll give up sweets for Lent if you help me get the job I want». They are not control techniques. The disciplines of the spiritual life, Jesus says, should be performed quietly and cheerfully and interiorly.

Secondly, Jesus emphasises verbal economy in prayer. We should not go «babbling on like the heathen who think the more they say the more likely they are to be heard». Quantity and length do not authenticate prayer because, as he tells us,

«Your Father knows what you need before you ask him».

Prayer is not informing God of our needs or asking God to change «his» mind. We are not setting up our will in opposition to God's will or telling God what he should be doing. Such egocentric prayer fosters many forms of neurotic religious behaviour, such as praying for victory over others or the fulfilling of our fantasies or egotistical desires. Absurdity of his kind begins by creating a God in our own ego image. It may then continue in the obsessive maintenance of a fantasy relationship with the false god of our making. Such a god can develop enough autonomous psychic life to close us to true divinity when it actually approaches. This can be just as dangerous spiritually as the way the demon of the ego weaves the illusion that we inhabit a personal reality separate and independent from God.

4

In the petitions of the Lord's Prayer we see how all prayer touches on human relationships no less than the root-relationship with God. The prayer shows the single web of consciousness that comprises knowledge of God, self-knowledge and relationship to others. If we have not forgiven those who sin against us we will never ourselves feel forgiven nor can we ever be free from the fear that God will punish us for our sins.

5

A third emphasis in Jesus' teaching on prayer concerns radical detachment from material anxieties. We cannot serve both the God who is Spirit and the god of materialism. And so, Jesus says, when you pray,

> «I bid you put away anxious thoughts about food and drink to keep you alive and clothes to cover your body».

In the Galilee of Jesus' time he was probably addressing not a band of starving peasants but an affluent and sophisticated audience. To tell the starving not to worry about food is not the same as telling it to the rich. Anxiety about material concerns does not mean a total disregard for the basic necessities of life. We need to eat and drink. Identifying the Self and true happiness with what goes extravagantly beyond basic needs is the problem. Liberation from desire and fear and developing inner and outer trust are the conditions of prayer according to the teaching of Jesus.

6

The fourth great emphasis of his teaching: pure attention to the power of God at the heart of all reality is summed up in these memorable words:

«Set your mind on God's kingdom and his justice before everything else, and all the rest will come to you as well».

By this mindfulness we are led into the dynamic pilgrimage at the heart of prayer, to the threshold of continuous prayer, into the stillness of here and the peace of now. He tells us,

«So, do not be anxious about tomorrow; tomorrow will look after it».

7

*

There are many other sayings and stories of Jesus which elaborate on the Sermon on the Mount's essential teaching on prayer. Often, for example, he emphasises the need for perseverance in prayer and its power to move the mountain of the ego and germinate the inner seed of the Kingdom. He spoke too about praying «in my name», a phrase which means «in my way». Or «in the way I do it». The Sermon on the Mount summarises prayer as a spiritual practice transcending egotism and therefore dissolving fear and transforming desire. It combines interiority, simplicity, trust, attention and being in the present moment.

# Meditation and the Lord's Teaching of Prayer

In the Lord's Prayer, we see Jesus' essential teaching on prayer.

1

How can we practise what he preached? How can we do all this simultaneously and naturally? There are many forms of prayer: petition, intercession, praise, the reading of scripture, liturgy and worship, discursive, devotional practice, and charismatic. We can pray on a solitary walk in the country by contemplating nature or by attending a solemn cathedral service with choir, incense and sermons. We pray with thanks for a happy birth, in sorrow for a peaceful death, in perplexity over misfortune, in distraction much of the time. All ways of prayer are valid; all are effective in their own way provided they proceed from a sincere heart.

However, the ordinary prayer of Christians has suffered from the loss of its contemplative dimension. Without this contemplative dimension, all these different forms tend to settle into an orbit around the ego of the person praying. This was my own experience and it led to a growing dissatisfaction with prayer in any form, a sense of being bored with God, a sense of inauthenticity. Without the contemplative dimension any form of prayer risks becoming merely formal: ritualistic, neurotic, compulsive, self-indulgent; exactly what Jesus warned us against in the Sermon on the Mount. Such forms of prayer can degenerate into little more than ways for a group to relate to itself or for an individual to apply a little self-therapy in the stress of life. They lose their transcendent potential in the Spirit, and lose touch with that communion with the loving ground of being which Jesus called his Father and our Father.

## 3

No one can judge the quality of another's prayer but the fruits of prayer are self-evident. If we pray as Jesus taught, we will live as he taught. This was clear to the early Christians who said, «The way you live is the way you pray». If prayer does not make a difference —if it does not first of all change the one praying first of all— then something is wrong.

# Recovering the Contemplative Dimension of Life

The burning question today for Christian faith is how can we recover the lost contemplative dimension of life? The way we pray is the way we live.

1
∽

Many Westerners have sought it in the East where the interiority of the spiritual life seems to be more instinctive. But many Christians seek in a Christian tradition for a contemplative prayer practice, to help them apply the teaching of Jesus in daily life and to pray «in his name».

2
∽

Such a practice has been tragically missing from Christian spiritual formation in modern times. Down the centuries, indeed, the deep roots of meditative practice have been marginalised in Christian life and largely forgotten. As a result, when they are recovered, they often create suspicion. The teachers of the religion were not taught how to meditate.

Yet a Christian way of meditation, simple and capable of being practised by all, is to be found in the teachings of the first Christian monks. A number of contemporary teachers have drawn attention to it. A modern Benedictine monk, John Main, recognised and recovered it from long practical neglect. His contemporary way of teaching it has helped a great many people of all ages and walks of life around the world to open up the contemplative dimension of their faith and their daily lives. Through his transmission of this tradition they have been enabled to play again the lost chord of Christian prayer. They have found, «through their own experience» as John Main liked to say, that they could verify, deepen and personalise the mysteries of their faith. The seed of their faith germinated through a prayer of the heart which has been practised by their fellow Christians from the beginning and has subtle links with the contemplative tradition in other faiths.

Over the past twenty years this dramatic rediscovery of Christian meditation has deepened the way many can understand their Christian identity. Until quite recently meditation or contemplation was considered the preserve of cloistered specialists. Lay people and others in the «active life» were considered either unsuitable or incapable of the greater depths of prayer. Today, however, through the influence of many Christian teachers, of whom the monks Henri le Saux, Thomas Merton, Bede Griffiths, Thomas Keating and John Main are exemplars, contemplative practice has been reclaimed as a universal dimension of Christian spirituality. It has changed rapidly from being seen as a monastic or clerical privilege to become the daily practice of lay people in all walks of life. These are now also its principal teachers as is evident in a contemplative network, The World Community for Christian Meditation, that grew from John Main's teaching.

In the early fifth century John Cassian, who had settled in southern France after absorbing the teaching of the Desert Fathers, compiled the authoritative distillation of their practical wisdom in his «Conferences of the Fathers». In the late 1960s John Main was able to recognise in their teaching on prayer the Christian practice of the mantra. He saw it as a sublimely simple and appropriate method of non-discursive meditation that allowed modern Christians to explore the full depths of their spirit in the unabashed light of their Christian faith and tradition. This is what Cassian says about the mantra which he calls in Latin a formula.

«The formula for this discipline and prayer that you are seeking shall be presented to you. Every monk who longs for the continual awareness of God should be in the habit of meditating on it ceaselessly in his heart, after having driven out every kind of thought, because he will be unable to hold fast to it in any other way than by being freed from all bodily cares and concerns. Just as this was handed down to us by a few of the oldest fathers who were left, so also we pass it on to none but the most exceptional, who truly desire it... This verse should be poured out in unceasing prayer so that we may be delivered in adversity and preserved and not puffed up in prosperity. You should meditate constantly on this verse in your heart... Let sleep overtake you as you meditate upon this verse until you are formed by having used it ceaselessly and are in the habit of repeating it even while asleep... Let the mind hold ceaselessly to this formula above all until it has been strengthened by constantly using and continually meditating upon it and until it renounces and rejects the whole wealth and abundance of thoughts. Thus, disciplined by the poverty of this verse it will very easily attain to that gospel beatitude which holds the first place among the other beatitudes: poverty of spirit».

That was John Cassian in the 10th Conference describing the meaning and the value of the mantra.

## 6

In his youth Main had learned to meditate with the
mantra from an Indian teacher whom he met and
studied briefly with in Malaya. What he learned by
word and example from his teacher enabled him to
see what Cassian actually meant in his tenth Conference when he emphasised so strongly the «continual repetition» in the heart of the formula drawn
from scripture.

7

Neither Cassian nor Main claimed that this was the
«only» or even the best way to meditate, certainly
not that it excluded other ways. They also both
recognised the variety, mysteriousness and fluidity
of prayer, and the supreme freedom of the Spirit
to lead us in wherever way it wishes. Cassian intro-
duces his magisterial Tenth Conference on the
mantra with the brilliant Ninth Conference which
describes the diversity as well as the unifying pur-

pose of prayer. Prayer has a direction. It is taking us somewhere. As a monk Main's own daily life, like Cassian's, was enriched by scripture, communal worship, Eucharistic liturgy and art.

8

But John Main and Cassian also saw, painful clearly, that the great problem in prayer is the complex and distracted mind. Without solving this, the forms of prayer can remain tragically superficial and so, even when practised with good intentions, can effect no deep transformation. Cassian and Main knew that this problem called for a remedy that was absolutely radical in its simplicity. In the traditional practice of the formula, or mantra, they saw how attention leads to simplicity. This led them to see further: in poverty of spirit union with the prayer of Jesus, who is perfectly attentive to the Father and to us who are praying, is realised. Our prayer is therefore taken up into his prayer.

## 9

John Main saw in Cassian's Christocentric teaching of the mantra that what modern people needed was an alternative and an antidote for their compulsive self-analysis. They needed a healing for the personal woundedness afflicting so many in our society. The mantra is not magic. It is not an easy practice to follow. But it is simple. And so complex a mentality as our own demands nothing less than a discipline of complete simplicity. It requires commitment and perseverance which are not congenial to the modern personality. But an increasing number of people sense that it is what they need, and put this into practice. Main, like Cassian and the fourteenth-century Cloud of Unknowing and many other teachers of this tradition, built their teaching on this insight into simplicity but without compromising its demanding authenticity. In a simple, direct and practical style John Main taught Christian meditation in a way that empowered others to discover the depth of the practice for themselves.

## 10

~∽~

I like to end this section with this quotation from John Main's book «Word Into Silence»

«As I have suggested, prayer is not a matter of talking to God, but of listening to Him, or being with Him. It is this simple understanding of prayer that lies behind John Cassian's advice that if we want to pray, to listen, we must become quiet and still, by reciting a short verse over and over again. Cassian received this method as something which was an old, established tradition in his own day and it is an enduring universal tradition… Let me repeat the basic method of meditation. Sit down comfortably, relax. Make sure you are sitting upright. Breathe calmly and regularly. Close your eyes and then in your mind and heart begin to repeat the word that you have chosen as your meditation word… Choosing your word, or mantra, is of some importance. Ideally, you should choose your mantra in consultation with your teacher. But there are various mantras which are possible for a beginner… Some of these words were first taken over as mantras for Christian meditation by the Church in its earliest days. One of these is the word *maranatha*. This is the mantra I recommend to most beginners, the Aramaic phrase *maranatha*, which means, "Come Lord. Come Lord Jesus"».

# The Journey of Meditation

Sitting down to meditate for the first time is a decisive moment in your spiritual path. It is similar to turning on the ignition at the beginning of a long car trip. What happens then? The journey simply begins. You pull away from the curb. Then like all journeys it proceeds by stages. There are delays, traffic jams, wrong turns, moments of exhaustion as well as the thrill of travel and the discovery of the new. These stages and their events could be described by means of a simple map of the levels of consciousness or as stages of self-knowledge unfolding through a gentle and steady discipline.

1

We begin at the beginning, on the surface. As soon as we begin to meditate we discover the first and superficial level of consciousness: restless, light-headed, undisciplined, distracted mental activity, rampant fantasy. It comes as something of a shock to realise just how uncontrolled and chaotic this level of mind actually is. In our culture we so rarely practise any conscious attention that when we do it seems strange and straining. A recent survey estimated that for most people attention span becomes difficult after anything longer than a television commercial.

2

Discovering our chronic distractedness can, at least initially, make meditation an upsetting and humiliating experience. Even if we think of ourselves as relatively calm and recollected, meditation soon disillusions us. The first step of self-knowledge clearly shows that our mind is neither stable nor clear. At this early stage the journey may seem to have ground to a halt before it has even begun. We have no choice but to accept that we are not nearly as capable of paying attention as we had thought. The shock of this discovery may undermine the will to persevere. It can be discouraging and it will certainly recur. But it helps to reflect that if we can see clearly that we are distracted then that very awareness itself is progress. Once recognized, confusion begins to clear. We begin to see the truly simple nature of meditation and to appreciate the challenge it presents.

The first level of self-knowledge is turbulent. Walter Hilton in the fourteenth century says, «It is like a man coming home from work to find a smoking fire and a nagging wife». The early Desert Fathers and mothers did not have domestic problems. But they were shocked to discover that, even in their desert hermitages, they were unable to abandon the anxieties, temptations and erotic fantasies of their former lives. Sitting with no external distraction they found themselves, like us today, bombarded by unrestrained mental activity, thinking or fantasising compulsively about everything they thought they had abandoned. They seethed at their brethren, condemning the lazy, envying the holier. They obsessed about the trivia of their manual labour of weaving mats or work in the fields. They became compulsive about their few material possessions. They fantasised about sex and even more, about food. Perhaps we are no more inherently distracted today then the monks of the desert or meditators in any time or culture. It just seems more difficult for us to get through the first phase.

### 4

Distraction and the craving for variety are endemic to the human mind. The ego is by nature restless in its quest for pleasure and the evasion of pain. The human mind today, however, is bombarded by image and information bytes as never before. Print and electronic media and the speed of communication accelerate the volume and intensity of distractedness. The average office worker is stressed merely by the number of daily e-mails. The hungry consumer mentality contributes added stress to mind and body. Information technology has perhaps even developed a new level of human consciousness, the collective media-consciousness. This has potential for unifying humanity but as great a danger of reducing the individual mind to a clone in the mass-mind. Advertising, gossip, information, news, chat, erotica, entertainment, stimulate minds from Hyderabad to Harwich with the same material. Cyberspace saturates us daily and we cry for more.

5

One of the fruits of meditation is the gift of discernment: about what the media is doing and saying to us, about when to switch off the screen. By creating the space of solitude through daily practice meditation protects the dignity of individual privacy. As a result of this it also develops the social values of personal liberty and responsible participation in society's decision-making. The passivity and fatalism that media-saturation can create is challenged by meditation, if only because people of wisdom are less easily misled.

6

We meditate in this world. Our decision to meditate represents a commitment to participate responsibly even in a world going mad. Meditation trains discernment and limits intolerance. Each time we sit to meditate we carry our own and the world's baggage into the work of attention. It is a way of loving the world we are part of and contributing to its well-being. Precisely because it is a way of letting go of ourselves meditation helps us to share the burden of humanity.

7

A capacity for wonder and a love of wisdom return with contemplative practice. Imperceptibly, over the years, exposure to the media can erode our capacity for direct experience. Increasingly we experience events and emotions secondhand, through the views of others or the cult of celebrity. This alienation from personal experience can turn our gift for empathy into apathy. We are rendered too unreal to serve others. Yet the media can also make us aware of the need for peace of mind. Distraction, alienation, frustration can stimulate us to undertake the contemplative journey. «Where sin is, grace abounds all the more», according to St Paul. Noise awakens the thirst for silence and this thirst is the global spirituality of our time.

# The Antidote for Worry and Anxiety

So, turning off phones, television, radio, computer and stereo we sit in silence and stillness to meditate. We take time to sit well —back straight, alert and relaxed. breathing regularly. The door is closed. The kids are being looked after. The files on our desk can wait. We have a precious half hour to be. We have entered into our inner room. We begin to say the word, the mantra. What happens next?

1

All hell breaks loose. The programming continues. Shreds of advertising jingles, subconsciously implanted images, fear-producing news stories, fantasies and nightmares all jumble around in the mind when we sit to meditate. In addition to what the media has delivered there are the zillion daily errands and transient problems of our personal lives. You sit to meditate and begin saying the mantra. Then immediately you remember you should have taken the car to the garage. And is my next appointment at three or four? Should I do the washing today or tomorrow? Wasn't that dinner guest's dress a beautiful colour last night? Hang on, I should be saying the mantra. Am I saying it properly? Is this really getting me anywhere? I wonder if you know when enlightenment happens. What is enlightenment? Where is God? Is God really in this? Am I wasting time? Is there a better way of doing it? I must decide whether to take the morning or evening flight from Boston. Where's the mantra gone now? Come on, back to it. How much longer is this going to last? Did I set the alarm properly? I'll take a quick look. A cup of coffee would be nice, if I've got time. This will be better when I make a retreat. It will be lovely to be just quiet and away. Then I'll be able to meditate well. Should I go for the full week I have off or keep a few days free for a holiday as well? What would John Main advise? Or the *Gita*? The *Bhagavad Gita* is wonderful. Mortality is a great teacher. Say your mantra. You're wasting precious time. Why does my side hurt after meals? My father died of cancer. I am going to start a low fat diet tomorrow. There are special products now at the supermarket for that. Did I get the new supermarket credit card? There are so many things to remember. Jesus said one thing is necessary. I wonder what it is. The alarm will go off any second now. Let's say the mantra from now till then. Oh I forgot to call... And so on.

**2**

In the Sermon on the Mount, Jesus identified material concerns as our main source of anxiety. How can we make ourselves more comfortable and reduce personal suffering? This is the major preoccupation which obscures the present moment and disrupts our true priorities. Jesus said,

> «Therefore I bid you put away anxious thoughts about food and drink to keep you alive, and clothes to cover your body. Surely life is more than food, the body more than clothes» (Mk 6:25).

When he tells us not to worry, Jesus is not denying the reality of daily problems. It is anxiety he is telling us to abandon, not reality. Learning not to worry is hard work. His teaching is that consciousness is more than the thoughts or feelings that occupy our concerns for the body. It is also soul and spirit. And so, despite its «attention-deficiency disorder», even the modern mind has also its natural capacity to be still and to transcend its fixations. In depth it discovers its own clarity where it is at peace, free from anxiety. Most of us have half-a-dozen or so favourite anxieties, like bitter sweets we suck on endlessly. We would be frightened to be deprived of them. Jesus challenges us to go beyond the fear of letting go of anxiety, the fear we have of peace itself. The practice of meditation is a way of applying his teaching on prayer; it proves through experience that the human mind can indeed choose not to worry.

3

This is not to say we can easily blank the mind and dispel all thoughts at will. In meditation we remain distracted and yet are free from distraction. This is because —however minimally at first— we are free to choose where to place our attention. Gradually the discipline of daily practice strengthens this freedom. It would be childish to imagine that this is fully realised in a short time. We stay distracted for a long time. We soon get used to distractions as travelling companions on the path of meditation. But they do not have to dominate us. Choosing to say the mantra faithfully and to keep returning to it whenever distractions intervene exercises the freedom we have to pay attention. It is not a choice in the sense in which we choose a particular brand off the supermarket shelf. It is the choice to commit, a choice to admit the truth.

4

The way of the mantra is an act of faith, not a movement of the ego's power. Within every act of faith, there is a declaration of love. Faith prepares the ground for the seed of the mantra to germinate in love. We do not create the miracle of life and growth by ourselves but we are responsible for its unfolding. Coming to peace of mind and heart —to silence, stillness and simplicity— requires not the will of a type-A high-achiever but the unconditional, sustained attention and fidelity of a disciple. It means learning to wait in hope, with heightened and certain expectancy but without demands and expectations. Jesus says

«Hold yourselves ready then because the Son of Man will come at the time you least expect him» (Luke 12:40).

5

Perseverance in stillness is the dynamic of prayer. The teaching of Jesus on prayer is proven through our own experience. It becomes pertinent to us personally as soon as we begin to meditate and try to persevere. When we face the surface distractions and anxieties, the spirit of discipleship begins to mature. By this work of attention, self-knowledge grows.

6

Until you meditate, meditation may seem a mind-game, abstract and cerebral. Once experienced it shows itself to be the most incarnate and holistic path of prayer. Its effects are felt in the whole person as the words of the gospel take flesh in daily life. The teaching of Jesus permeates everything. What happens in and to us, our own experience, becomes the medium of seeing and recognising him. As John Main said, meditation verifies the truths of faith.

7

Meditation is a journey of awakening. Practised in faith, we see that it is the journey hidden within the visible journey of life. To meditate then is simply to be human. To meditate as a Christian is to see that by descending into the centre of our being we discover, in relationship and in the communion of the Spirit, who Jesus is.

*The Goal of Life*

This book was printed on *thin opaque smooth white Bible paper,* using the *Minion* and *Type Embellishments One* font families.

This edition was printed in D'VINNI, S.A., in Bogotá, Colombia, during the last weeks of the fourth month of year two thousand twelve.

*Ad publicam lucem datus mensis aprilis,
festivitatem Divina Misericordia*